Guestbook

Date

Our Guests

Messages and Wishes

_____

_____

_____

_____

_____

Our Guests

Messages and Wishes

Our Guests

Messages and Wishes

Our Guests

Messages and Wishes

Our Guests

Messages and Wishes

Our Guests

Messages and Wishes

Our Guests

Messages and Wishes

Our Guests

Messages and Wishes

Our Guests

Messages and Wishes

Our Guests

Messages and Wishes

Our Guests

Messages and Wishes

Our Guests

Messages and Wishes

Our Guests

Messages and Wishes

Our Guests

Messages and Wishes

Our Guests

Messages and Wishes

Our Guests

Messages and Wishes

Our Guests

Messages and Wishes

Our Guests

Messages and Wishes

Our Guests

Messages and Wishes

Our Guests

‖– –‖‖– –‖

‖– –‖‖– –‖

‖– –‖‖– –‖

‖– –‖‖– –‖

‖– –‖‖– –‖

Messages and Wishes

Our Guests

Messages and Wishes

Our Guests

Messages and Wishes

Our Guests

Messages and Wishes

Our Guests

Messages and Wishes

Our Guests

Messages and Wishes

Our Guests

Messages and Wishes

Our Guests

Messages and Wishes

Our Guests

Messages and Wishes

Our Guests

Messages and Wishes

Our Guests

Messages and Wishes

Our Guests

Messages and Wishes

Our Guests

Messages and Wishes

Our Guests

Messages and Wishes

Our Guests

Messages and Wishes

Our Guests

Messages and Wishes

Our Guests

Messages and Wishes

Our Guests

Messages and Wishes

Our Guests

Messages and Wishes

Our Guests

Messages and Wishes

Our Guests

Messages and Wishes

Our Guests

Messages and Wishes

Our Guests

Messages and Wishes

Our Guests

Messages and Wishes

Our Guests

Messages and Wishes

Our Guests

Messages and Wishes

Our Guests

Messages and Wishes

Our Guests

Messages and Wishes

Our Guests

Messages and Wishes

Our Guests

Messages and Wishes

Our Guests

Messages and Wishes

Our Guests

Messages and Wishes

Our Guests

Messages and Wishes

Our Guests

Messages and Wishes

Our Guests

Messages and Wishes

Our Guests

Messages and Wishes

Our Guests

Messages and Wishes

Our Guests

Messages and Wishes

Our Guests

Messages and Wishes

Our Guests

Messages and Wishes

Our Guests

Messages and Wishes

Our Guests   *Messages and Wishes*

Our Guests

Messages and Wishes

Our Guests

Messages and Wishes

Our Guests

Messages and Wishes

Our Guests

Messages and Wishes

Our Guests

Messages and Wishes

Our Guests

Messages and Wishes

Our Guests

Messages and Wishes

Our Guests

Messages and Wishes

Our Guests

Messages and Wishes

Our Guests

Messages and Wishes

Our Guests

_____

_____

_____

_____

_____

Messages and Wishes

Our Guests

Messages and Wishes

Our Guests

Messages and Wishes

THANK YOU!

WE HOPE YOU ENJOYED OUR BOOK!

As a small family company, your feedback is very important for us!

Please let us know what your experience with our book was at:

loocianabooks@gmail.com

Lightning Source UK Ltd.
Milton Keynes UK
UKHW030714110121
376834UK00011B/1379